W9-ALT-980

STRAHOV
Monastery

Strahov Monastery with the Church of the Assumption of Our Lady
illuminated on a romantic evening

Brief History
of
STRAHOV

P rince of Bohemia Vladislav and Jindřich Zdík, Bishop of Olomouc, founded a monastery in a place called Strahov in 1140. Members of the Premonstratensian Order have resided here since 1143.

Premonstratensians, who arrived in Prague from Steinfeld in Rhineland, began to build the monastery under the leadership of Abbot Gezo; it was wooden initially, only replaced with stone buildings later. Bishop Zdík hallowed the foundations of the new church in 1143; the construction was swift and apparently completed at the turn of the 1150s. Structural modifications in the chancel and the installation of a new altar called for a repeated consecration of the church, which was done in 1182. The original Romanesque disposition of the monastery was complete by then.

The early 13th century brought hard times for Strahov Monastery. The warfare among the Přemyslid dynasty had an impact on Strahov. At the same time, internal discord among the community members contributed substantially to the decline of the monastery. The latter half of the 13th century was better: Archbishop Conrad of Cologne – a papal legate – lodged in Strahov during his stay in Prague, and King of Bohemia Přemysl Otakar II summoned a congress there.

The promising upswing of the monastery was broken off by a fire on 19 October 1258, caused by the candle of a careless brother and wreaking considerable damage on the church and the monastic buildings. Abbot Jan

The towers of the Church of the Assumption of Our Lady raise above
the prelature and convent roofs

The Strahov Monastery entrance gate is crowned with a statue
of St. Norbert by Jan Antonín Quittainer

was repairing the buildings for five years. The monastery was plundered during the Brandeburg invasion and as soon as it recovered, it was looted again by Carinthian mercenaries. Peace was re-established only when the Luxembourgs ascended to the throne of Bohemia. It did not last long, because the Hussite movement dealt a hard blow to Strahov. The Hussites occupied the monastery on 8 May 1420 and despoiled it. Led by the abbot, the community managed to flee, only finding refuge in Bresslau. The church and the monastic buildings were severely damaged by fire after the loot. The library,

the sacral vestments, the books – everything was reduced to ashes.

The period between 1420 and 1586, when Jan Lohelius would assume the abbatial throne, brought hard times for the monastery. After the war turmoil subsided and the canons regular returned home – to a ruined monastery – a struggle for existence rather than religious life awaited them. Since the monastic possessions had been pillaged, funding for repairs was deficient. The dissatisfactory state of the community, lack of young members, low level of education among the community, and the risk of the monastery falling into

The 12th century hall – originally the *cellarium* – is among the oldest extant Romanesque components of the Strahov Monastery

Utraquist hands: all this led to the fact that abbots from other Bohemian and Moravian Premonstratensian monasteries were enthroned at Strahov. The entire 15th and 16th centuries saw efforts to elevate the Strahov Monastery to its former glory, but those efforts failed due to the social circumstances as well as the personal qualities of some of the prelates.

Only Jan Lohelius' ascent to the abbatial throne brought a reversal. Originally a canon regular from Teplá, he became Strahov Abbot in 1586, investing all his capacities in renewing Strahov. He strove for an improvement in the religious life of the monastery, and being the visitator of the circary as well as the entire Premonstratensian Order in Bohemia, he took heed of the material aspect too. He rebuilt the church and monastery buildings and recovered much of the stolen possessions, renewing the material base of the monastery. Lohelius' immense effort and tireless activity are best documented by the fact that a community of twelve brethren were able to live in Strahov as soon as 1594.

Jan Lohelius became Archbishop of Prague in 1612; the new Abbot Kašpar Questenberg resumed his work at Strahov. He continued the large-scale rebuilding initiated by Lohelius, completing the lower cloisters and the prelature, erecting a new St. Elizabeth's

The statue of St. Norbert by Jan Antonín Quittainer in the facade niche of the provisoriate building

The cloisters around the paradise garden command an unusual
view of the Strahov Church towers

The cloisters contain illusional paintings of scenes
from the life of St. Norbert

The mass has been prepared in the Strahov Church vestry with rich
pictorial decoration and 17th century furnishings to this day

hospital, outbuildings, a brewery, and establishing the Norbertinum college in the Old Town of Prague, intended for theological studies of the order members. All of this took place during the Thirty Years' War, when he himself had to flee Prague to avoid violence.

It was under his office as abbot that one of the greatest events of the Premonstratensian history took place: the transfer of the bodily remains of the founder of the order, St. Norbert, from Magdeburg to Strahov. This was in 1627, since when the body of the founding saint has rested in Strahov church. Questenberg also completed St. Roch's Church, originally a votive one, commissioned by Emperor Rudolph II in 1602 as a way of thanking for the forfending of a plague in 1599. After much difficulty, St. Roch's Church was completed, including the interior, in 1630.

The winter refectory with the painting *'Christ after Lent Served by Angels'*
by Jan Jiří Heinsch, dating from 1684

When Questenberg died in 1640, Kryšpín Fuk became the Abbot; he continued the work and won renown for making the St. John's Rapids on the Vltava river navigable. Swedish soldiery looted the monastery during his office towards the end of the Thirty Years' War. Both the church and the library were despoiled. After the Swedes left, Abbot Fuk, succeeded by Abbots Amelunxen and Sutor, restored the damaged monastery. Abbot Franck rebuilt the prelature and built the new St. Elizabeth's hospital, as the original one, built by Questenberg, had to make way for the new Baroque fortification of Prague.

Siard Nosecký's fresco 'Heavenly Feast of the Just with Christ as the Host', painted on the summer refectory ceiling between 1728–1731

Jeroným Hirnheim, a thinker and a theologist, became the Abbot in 1670. His years in office are memorialised by the library hall (present-day Theological Hall), which he had built. Abbots of the 17th and early 18th centuries continued rebuilding the monastery in the Baroque style; the summer refectory was erected, the brewery refurbished, and the outbuildings developed. The church was repaired and redecorated several times.

St. Norbert close up in the summer
refectory lectorium

The monastery underwent one more extensive restoration after the invasion of French and Bavarian armies in Prague in 1742: it had been bombed out. Both the church and the monastic buildings were rebuilt in recovery from the damage suffered. Václav Mayer became the Abbot in 1779: the last great builder on the abbatial throne. His greatest achievement was the construction of the new library: present-day Philosophical Hall.

The richly decoratively carved lectorium in the summer refectory and the picture of the founder of Strahov, Bishop Jindřich Zdík

Altar to St. Hermann Joseph with a painting
by Petr Molitor in the chapterhouse

The chapterhouse with paintings portraying
the Premonstratensian saints

That was the end of the centuries-long lively construction activity in Strahov Monastery; only period modifications followed. The monastery retained its late 18th century appearance until 1950, when it was confiscated by the Communist regime and the members of the community were interned, posted to civil occupations or enlisted in military service. The monastic premises were then subjected to an extensive archaeological survey, which rediscovered its Romanesque form. The res-

The Calvary group in front of the former St. Elizabeth's hospital, part of the monastery compound

toration, done in line with the period's conservationist and artistic policy, combined the oldest unearthed architectural elements with the Baroque and later modifications. The newly constituted Museum of Czech Literature was located in the Strahov Monastery.

The new political circumstances of 1989 brought changes to Strahov, too. The monastery was restored to the Premonstratensian Order and rebuilding works resumed. The former offices of the Museum of Czech Literature once again serve their original pur-

pose: canons' quarters. Dissatisfactory utility networks were renovated, the picture gallery was restored, and the restitution of the library commenced. Monastery gardens were tidied, and the church restoration was completed. The monastery invested a great deal of funds and efforts in other restored buildings in Jihlava, Milevsko, Svatý Kopeček near Olomouc, and Doksany, where the semale Premonstratensian community was renewed that had ceased to exist when Emperor Joseph II disbanded monasteries.

The Gothic-Renaissance St. Roch's Church in Strahov Courtyard was designed by the architect Giovanni Maria Filippi and built in the 17th century

STRAHOV
Church

Having climbed the stairs from Pohořelec to Strahov Courtyard, one sees
the Church of the Assumption of Our Lady and the provisoriate frontage

The Abbey church was built as a Romanesque three-aisled basilica with a flat wooden ceiling and a transept, with three equal open apses in the east. Its towers stood essentially where the existing ones are. After a devastating fire in 1258, the church was given a vault and underwent some Early Gothic modifications. The St. Ursula's Chapel was added along the northern wall: it was the only place fit for church services after the church and the monastery were looted by the Hussites.

Following a long period of decline, the church only began thriving again under Abbot Jan Lohelius. His reconstruction gave the church a Late Gothic to Renaissance appearance.

The next Strahov Abbot Kašpar Questenberg, who took the office after Lohelius' departure to the Prague Archbishopric, had the church extended by some seven metres westwards and new frontage built, of which the main portal remains to this day. He ordered the Chapel of Our Lady of Passau added to the southern aisle, where the Chapel of Holy Guardian Angels used to stand. That was the appearance until 1742, when the church was bombed out during the French occupation of Prague. The battle did damage to the towers, the St. Ursula's Chapel, the vault and the church frontage. The ensuing final Baroque exterior modification, overseen probably by the Italian architect Anselmo Lurago, resulted in the present-day appearance of the church.

In spite of all the disasters that befell the church, all the modifications and rebuilds, the interior is a showcase of a uniform, sober Baroque style. The nave, rendered in soft colours, 63 metres long, 10 metres wide and 16 metres tall, is dominated by the main altar. The marble structure was made by Josef Lauermann in 1768 as well as the ten side altars of Slivenec marble, positioned along the pillars separating the side aisles from the nave. A gilded carving depicting the Assumption of Our Lady and the Holy Trinity adorns the centre of the main altar. The sanctuary, made in 1873, is flanked by gilded wooden larger--than-life statues portraying St. Augustine and the Premonstratensian Saints Norbert, Gottfried and Hermann Joseph. They were made by Ignác Platzer in 1768.

The group statue 'Betrothal of St. Hermann Joseph with the Virgin Mary' by Jan Antonín Quittainer at the St. Norbert's Chapel

The expansive Strahov Courtyard is dominated by the Basilica of the Assumption of Our Lady.
Its present-day Baroque appearance dates from the mid–18th century, when the architect
Anselmo Lurago supervised the reconstruction of the church, damaged in battle

The St. Norbert's Chapel is a precious part of the church: it holds the saint's remains.
Formerly it was consecrated to St. Ursula, whose statue adorns the chapel gable

The Epistle side of the presbytery holds an epitaph dated 1727, dedicated to the founders of Strahov; another one from 1626, commemorating the renewer of the monastery Abbot Jan Lohelius, is located on the Gospel side. Moreover, the presbytery contains richly carved chancel pews from Abbot Questenberg's times, and a small organ made in 1685 to accompany the canons regular during choir singing.

The chancel is separated from the nave with a marble balustrade, decorated with a gilded wrought-iron grille, which bears wooden sculptures made by Ignác Platzer in 1747. Similar grilles, though without sculptures, decorate the entrances to the side chapels and the stairs to the marble pulpit, which is remarkable for its gilded rocaille carvings, reliefs of the four Evangelists with their attributes, and a carving of the Lamb from St. John's Apocalypse. Apart from the main altar, the Strahov Basilica has fourteen other altars, ten of which are situated along the pillars

The stucco cartouches on the nave walls hold twelve frescoes
with scenes from the life of St. Norbert

separating the side aisles from the nave. Each opposing pair was made in an identical style. Michael Leopold Willman, Jan Kryštof Liška, and František Xaver Palko made the paintings on them; Jan Antonín Quittainer made the statues.

The new worship area, designed to suit the revised liturgy of the Second Vatican Council, is situated in front of the balustrade dividing the presby-tery from the nave. Egino Weinert of Cologne made the bronze altar in the early 1990s.

A chapel, enclosed with a wrought-iron grille, used to stand in front of the altar grille; it held the remains of the founder of the Premonstratensian Order, St. Norbert, transferred to Strahov from Magdeburg in 1627. The chapel, with a huge gilded wooden crown hung over it, was also damaged

Lohelius Jan Oehlschlägel built the grand organ for the church between 1764–1774; Wolfgang Amadeus Mozart himself appreciated its quality

The Gospel side of the church presbytery houses a small organ made in 1685;
the marble epitaph nearer the altar commemorates the outstanding Strahov Abbot
and Archbishop of Prague, Jan Lohelius

by the cannonade during the French-Bavarian invasion, and was ultimately removed in 1811.

The western end of the basilica is occupied by the organ-loft with a organ, built by the Strahov Premonstratensian Lohelius Jan Oehlschlägel between 1764–1774. It is of interest that Wolfgang Amadeus Mozart him-self appreciated its quality, when he improvised on it while visiting Strahov in 1787.

The inlaid confessionals, situated in the side aisles, were made by the Strahov laic brother Šimon Truska in 1783; Viktor Foerster made the Stations of the Cross with paintings in Art Nouveau colours in 1910. The

Michael Leopold Willman, Jan Kryštof Liška, and František Xaver Palko
made the paintings on the ten side altars

pews in the nave and the northern aisle were carved by the Strahov laic brother Melichar Elgass in 1706.

The Chapel of the Virgin Mary of Passau opens off the southern aisle. Its wooden altar dates from 1677; it bears a copy of the painting of the dear Virgin Mary which is kept to this day at the Cathedral in Innsbruck. The display case on the altar and the altar mensa hold the remains of St. Deodatus and St. Victor, respectively, both early Christian martyrs. Under the chapel is the burial chamber of General Pappenheim, a renowned warrior of the Thirty Years' War, who died in consequence of serious wounds received at the Battle of Lützen, 1632.

The Baroque pulpit in the church nave is decorated with reliefs of Evangelists and their attributes, and the carving of the Lamb from St. John's Apocalypse

The 19th century stained-glass window behind the altar in the St. Norbert's Chapel depicts St. Norbert alongside the venerable Ricuera and the beatified Hugo

St. Norbert's Chapel: the remains of the founder of the Premonstratensian Order
are kept in the gilded Classicist sarcophagus on the main altar of the chapel

A magnificent work of art close up: the altar grille with angels,
separating the chancel from the nave

The fresco *'Christ Before Pontius Pilate'* by Siard Nosecký decorates
the vault of the Holy Cross Chapel

His valiant feats are commemorated by the epitaph on the eastern chapel wall, dating from 1861.

A St. Catherine's Chapel probably used to stand by the southern aisle, as suggested by the ceiling fresco by the Strahov canon regular Siard Nosecký. The entrance to the vestry is located there now. The vestry has an altar to Our Lady Queen of Angels and carved oaken wardrobes made in 1633.

The northern aisle ends in the Holy Cross Chapel with a marble altar made in 1772 and a Baroque 'Ecce Homo' sculpture. The fresco 'Christ Before Pontius Pilate' by Siard Nosecký decorates the chapel ceiling.

All the church furnishings have been intended not only as period artistic expressions, but primarily as complements and decoration of the worship area to induce the believers' devoutness. That holds absolutely for the pictorial decoration as well. Looking up, you can admire the vault decorated by Jiří Vilém Neunhertz in 1744: its eight large and

The epitaph over the burial chamber of Imperial Marshal General Gottfried Heinrich Pappenheim in the Chapel of Our Lady of Passau

The chapel is overlooked by a copy of the painting
of Our Dear Lady of Passau made in 1677

The Epistle side of the presbytery holds an epitaph
to the founders of Strahov Monastery

thirty-two small fields depict scenes from the Lorettonian litanies and office antiphons on the Immaculate Conception of the Virgin Mary, which is revered traditionally by the Premonstratensian Order. Magnificent stucco cartouches by Ignác Palliardi, lining the walls of the nave, contain twelve frescoes by Jiří Vilém Neunhertz, showing scenes from the life of St. Norbert.

The chapel adjoining the northern aisle is consecrated to St. Norbert. A Gothic St. Ursula Chapel used to stand there originally, which was later rebuilt in the Baroque style. The previous consecration is suggested both by the Baroque statue of the martyr saint on the northern chapel gable, visible from the courtyard, and the St. Ursula Altar with a pyramidal display case inside the chapel. The glazed case holds the remains of female martyrs, helpers of St. Ursula, which

Archbishop Conrad of Cologne donated to Strahov when visiting in 1256. The altar mensa holds the remains of St. Exuperantius, transferred from St. George Basilica in Prague Castle. The Baroque marble baptismal font next to the St. Ursula Altar dates from 1773.

The remains of the founder of the Premonstratensian Order, St. Norbert, were originally deposited in the grille chapel in the centre of the church, and moved to the main altar after the former was removed. Abbot Vojtěch Hron had the St. Ursula Chapel converted in 1873. The remains of St. Norbert were transferred there, and the chapel renamed to St. Norbert's. The body of the founder of the Order is deposited on the altar, inside a coffin of exotic wood with wrought-silver reliefs, resting in a Classicist gilded sarcophagus made in 1811.

The Premonstratensians hold the Virgin Mary in particular reverence:
her numerous portraits are found throughout the monastery

PREMONSTRATENSIAN ORDER
and Its Mission

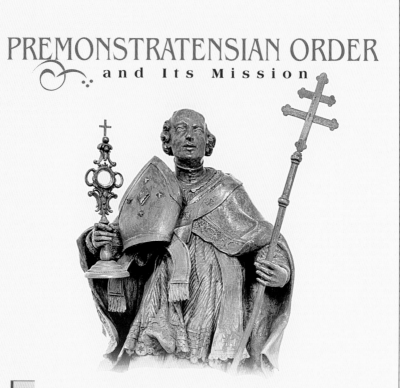

T he beginning of the second millennium was a period of reformist religious movements, associated with the growth of monasteries as centres of spiritual and intellectual life, appearance of outstanding sacred buildings and intense Christianisation in Europe. However, the link between religion and secular power led to a contest for investiture (i.e., whether representatives of either secular or clerical power were entitled to decide about religious superiors), nepotism (filling of clerical offices with relatives), and simony (trade in clerical offices and ranks). It was these vices that the reformists fought.

Norbert of Xanten, the founder of the Premonstratensian Order, was an outstanding reformer of that time. Advised to do so by friends, he founded a new order in Prémontré near Laon, France, in 1120. The order expanded all over Europe in his lifetime. Premonstratensians arrived in Bohemia thanks to Jindřich Zdík, Bishop of Olomouc, supported substantially by Prince Vladislav II and his wife Gertrude.

In 1126, Norbert was replaced as the head of the order by his clos-

A statue of St. Norbert, the founder of the Premonstratensian Order, in the home chapel of St. Mary Magdalene

est complice, Hugo de Fosses, who became the Abbot of Prémontré in 1128. His principal task was to impress a uniform structure on the order. Until then, the individual communities were more or less autonomous. Hugo established an uniform organisation and structure of the order, managed by general chapters. The General Abbot – synonymous to the Abbot of Prémontré until the French Revolution – was the head of the order. A general chapter met at Prémontré annually and discussed current issues of the order.

The order was divided into circaries (groupings of monasteries according to regional or linguistic criteria). The General Abbot exerted a legal power over all the circaries. The division into circaries has existed to this day alongside the fundamental elements of the order structure.

As in the overall church history, successive periods of prosperity, decline and subsequent growth can be seen in the history of the Premonstratensian Order.

The Order saw the greatest expansion before the 14th century, when

The life of the monastic community
revolves around Eucharist

monasteries contributed to the enhancement of both religious and cultural life near and far with their quantity, quality of life, and activities.

A crisis occurred within the Order in the 15th and 16th centuries, caused by both external drivers (Hussite Wars in Bohemia, reformation) and internal ones (declining communal life, installation of sometimes inappropriate superiors – the so-called commendatory abbots). Some circaries were given the rights of general chapters in the 17th century, which resulted in a dilution of the centralised power within the Order. Yet the period before the last quarter of the 18th century may be viewed as stabilised.

Premonstratensians faced an extensive process of disbandment of monasteries in the following decades: they were destroyed forcibly in France during the Revolution (Prémontré was disbanded in 1790); the Habsburg Monarchy saw the harsh religious reforms of Joseph II; secularisation took place in Germany as part of the war reparations in the early 19th century.

Only nine monasteries (including five in the Austrian Empire) and six convents remained of the Order after 1835. However, efforts to renew the Order and monastic life took place in that period. Not all of the efforts succeeded, yet monastic life was restored in Belgium, France, Germany and elsewhere. The uniformity of the Order was restored thanks to Popes Pius IX and Leo XIII.

The solemn liturgy is one of the basic characteristics of the Premonstratensian way of life

Abbot Michael Josef Pojezdný censing sacrificial
presents during Holy Mass

Despite minor difficulties, the late 19th and the first half of the 20th century were a period of growth for the Premonstratensians in Bohemia and Moravia. The canons regular managed to survive the Second World War (some were imprisoned and some died in concentration camps); the Communist regime was a much greater disaster. All male monasteries in the Czechoslovakia were disbanded forcibly in 1950; many Premonstratensians were unjustly condemned in false show trials. Strahov Abbot Bohuslav Jarolímek died in prison. The communities continued their work underground with more or less success, so that they could return to monasteries after 1989 and launch a restoration of the Order. The Order tradition, no doubt a rich one, continues again at present.

The vitality of the Premonstratensian Order is attested by its active missions in Africa, South America, and India, supported by European and

The recreation room, serving both relaxation
and social life in the monastery

The monastery's home chapel, consecrated
to St. Mary Magdalene

North American monasteries. At the moment, the Order has about 1,330 brothers and 374 sisters.

The Strahov Canonry has 78 members at present; 21 brothers now live directly at the monastery. The majority work in Bohemian and Moravian parishes (Premonstratensians operate the Jihlava Parish and the pilgrimage site of Svatý Kopeček near Olomouc, for example) as well as some in Slovakia. The Canonry also includes two dependent houses in Milevsko (South Bohemia) and Holíč (Slovakia); we also execute religious administration in the restored Premonstratensian convent in Doksany. Abbot Michael Josef Pojezdný is the head of the Canonry.

Our Spirituality

We are doing our best to make our lives service to God. We wish that our faith be live, our hope be firm, and our love ever growing. We find a joyful meaning of life in service to God.

This means to us that we wish to live according to the commandments of love for God and our neighbours.

Some may regard the principles ruling our lives too vague and may question their originality. Indeed, the subject matter is general – Catholic in the best sense – but the method of fulfilling it is Premonstratensian.

Our lives can be summarised in five articles:

Modern technologies have found their way
into the monastery: the scriptorium

Liturgical Life

Our primary mission is a common, public Prayer of the Church and eucharistic liturgy. This also follows from the reality of our canonical disposition. Prayer has priority over everything else. We seek to make it beautiful and, above all, dear to God.

Ascetic Life

This means observing certain restrictions, adhering to order, and enduring the vices of others with patience. We maintain a reserved position on ostentatious, paraded severity.

Apostolic Life

We guard against harmful individualism. We work as a community of brethren and sisters. We realise that prayer is part of any outward work, to obtain the fruit of God's blessing.

Eucharistic Life

We aim for all manner of outward and inward eucharistic reverence, directing it towards the holy mass. We strive to prevent any weakening of eucharistic reverence and the faith in Christ's real presence in the Sacrament. We gladly remain before the Eucharist and take care of accurate observation of liturgical rules.

Marian Life

The Virgin Mary is our Lady and Queen of our Order. She gave us the white vesture and most of our churches are consecrated to her. Mary is the maternal heart of our Order.

The home library, used by the canons regular, commands a beautiful view of the Prague Castle and the St. Vitus, Wenceslas and Adalbert's Cathedral

STRAHOV
Library

S trahov Library is the Czech Republic's second oldest church library in uninterrupted operation, and the country's third most valued one. Its collection encompasses some 250,000 volumes. There are about 3,000 manuscripts and 2,000 incunabula. The Strahov Evangeliary, originating from ca. 860, is undoubtedly one of the oldest and most precious manuscripts. Many of the other manuscripts and first prints are unique rarities. The library has oper-

ated as a scientific institution to that day, featuring its own catalogue and study, open to all scholars focusing on theology, history, auxiliary sciences of history, and history of art.

Visitors may view the two library halls and the northern connecting corridor between them. The Italian architect Giovanni Domenico Orsi built the older hall – the Theological Hall – under Abbot Jeroným Hirnheim. The fresco decoration is more recent: it was made by Strahov Pre-

The 9th century Strahov Evangeliary is one of the most precious manuscripts in the Strahov Library collection

monstratensian Siard Nosecký between 1721–1727. The scenes from the Books of Wisdom, Proverbs, Psalms and the New Testament on the relationship between wisdom, cognition and knowledge confronted with faith and religion are based on a philosophical-theological treatise by Abbot Hirnheim.

The interior of the Theological Hall, containing approximately 16,000 volumes of theological literature, is decorated with a collection of 17th to 19th century therrestrial and coelestial globes, largely of Dutch making. The compilation wheel, commissioned by Abbot Hirnheim in 1678, deserves special attention. There is also a Late Gothic statue of St. John the Evangelist, holding a girdle book on which the interesting medieval pouch binding is used.

Two parallel corridors connect the Theological and Philosophical Halls. The one open to visitors contains a collection of legal, medical and pharm-

One of the rich collection of 17th to 19th century therrestrial and coelestial globes, situated in the Theological Hall

The Theological Hall of the Strahov Library: the Gothic statue
of St. John the Evangelist, holding a girdle book

The stucco and fresco decoration of the Theological Hall: the Libri Prohibiti
used to be locked up over the entrances

Siard Nosecký's fresco *'Explication of the True Wisdom'*, painted on
the Theological Hall ceiling between 1721–1727

The self-portrait of the Strahov Premonstratensian painter
Siard Nosecký is situated in the Theological Hall

aceutical literature. It also has a remarkable dendrological library dating from 1825, comprising 68 volumes documenting woody plants growing in Bohemia. Each volume deals with one tree species: the spine is covered with its bark and the volume details the growth of the tree from the root to boughs, branches, leaves, blossoms and fruits. The eastern end of the corridor is decorated with an illusional painting, in front of which is the facsimile of the binding of the Strahov Evangeliary, made in the 1970s.

The Cabinet of Curiosities – a prototype of modern-day natural and art history museum – is situated in front of the Philosophical Hall. It grew from Baron Eben's collection, purchased by

Close-up of the decorated book cabinets in the Theological Hall and an early 17th century cancional of the Strahov Premonstratensians

the monastery in 1798. It encompasses archaeological finds, natural collections, glassware, chinaware, handicraft items, arms, a model of a 17th century warship, etc.

The tour of the Strahov Library concludes in the Philosophical Hall. Abbot Mayer had the detached hall built to house the new additions to the monastic library. The building was erected between 1783–1786, but the Abbot lacked the money to buy the bookshelves, so it remained empty. The Premonstratensian monastery in Louka near Znojmo was disbanded at that time, so Abbot Mayer bought the book cabinets for his new library from there. When they arrived, however, it was

The southern corridor connecting the Theological and Philosophical Halls
contains a handicraft collection in late 18th century cabinets

found that their dimensions did not match the existing library building. Abbot Mayer had two options: either adjust the cabinets, or rebuild the library. He chose the latter: he had the new building reconstructed to fit the book cabinets. Everything was ready in 1792. In 1794, the Viennese painter Franz Anton Maulbertsch painted the library ceiling, and master cabinetmarker Jan Lahofer of Tasovice, who had made the book cabinets, installed them.

The Philosophical Hall is 32 metres long, 10 metres wide, and 14 metres tall. The beautiful carved book cabinets hold about 50,000 volumes in many scientific disciplines (mathematics, physics, astronomy, history, art) as well as fiction, poetry and encyclopaedias. The case inlaid with mother-of-pearl in the centre of the hall contains ten volumes, donated by Marie Louise, the wife of Napoleon I, in 1813 after having visited the monastery. They are Les Liliacéés by J. P. Redoute and the Musée français by Crozé-Magnan. The noteworthy collapsible desk, containing a chair and steps, was commissioned in the late 18th century.

Close-up of the richly decoratively carved book cabinets in the Philosophical Hall

The Philosophical Hall cabinet containing the books donated to the Strahov
Library by Marie Louise, the second wife of Napoleon I

Franz Anton Maulbertsch painted the Philosophical Hall ceiling mural
'*Spiritual Advancement of Mankind*' al secco in 1794

Close-up of the Philosophical Hall ceiling mural,
portraying the Old Testament

The ceiling mural *'Spiritual Advancement of Mankind'*
in the Philosophical Hall

Franz Anton Maulbertsch included Abbot Mayer, the builder of the Philosophical Hall, among the Church Fathers and the patron Saints of Bohemia

The collection of curiosities in the Strahov
Library connecting corridor

Cabinet of Curiosities: a case containing
various sea animals

The inlaid book wheel in the Theological Hall is one of the most
attractive pieces of furniture in the Strahov Library

The ceiling painting by Anton Maulbertsch is an Enlightenment-inspired portrait of the human advancement and path towards the realisation of the Truth. The triumph of the Divine Providence is in the centre, while the sides depict the history of mankind. In the painter's perception, it had two milestones: the first is the Old Testament, represented by Moses and the Ten Commandments tablets. Around him stand characters of the Old Testament: Adam and Eve, Solomon, David, Aaron, Melchisedech, and others. The opposite side shows the other milestone in the human history: Christianity, represented by Apostle Paul at the Areopagus by an altar consecrated to an Unknown God. In addition, the Christian world is represented by a group of Church Fathers, patron Saints Ludmila, Wenceslas, John of Nepomuk, Norbert, and many other personalities, including the builder of the hall, Abbot Mayer. In between the two poles are the portraits of outstanding figures of the human history alongside mythological scenes and figures: Alexander the Great, Aristotle, Diogenes, Socrates, Galen, Asclepius, Plato, Democritus, and many other exponents of ancient wisdom. Due to the social circumstances, which had condemned the French Enlightenment as the cause of Revolution, they were portrayed as the prototypes of reprobate rationalists.

Exhibits in the Cabinet
of Curiosities

STRAHOV
Picture
Gallery

T he art-loving Abbot Jeroným II Zeidler founded the Strahov Picture Gallery in 1834; originally, it was situated in the seclusion, so it was inaccessible to the ordinary visitor. Its new installation on the first floor of the cloisters now allows the general public to view selections from the monastery's art collections.

Since its foundation, the monastery has collected works of art for the decoration of both the sacral areas and the monastery interiors. The Picture Gallery was only founded and organised systemically under Abbot Zeidler. Nowadays, the collection contains over one thousand and five hundred paintings; only some are accessible to the visitor, as many continue to decorate the seclusion. The works on display in the Gallery are a cross-section of the art of the 14th to 19th centuries. The plentiful Gothic collection is dominated by the 14th century Strahov Madonna,

The Central European Master of the 17th Century painted the doubting Thomas.
Jan Jiří Hering painted St. Augustine and St. Jerome

14th and 15th century Gothic Madonnas

Paintings by 19th century masters Ludvík Kohl, August Piepenhagen and
F. Hugo Seykora are part of the Strahov Picture Gallery collection

The Doksany Ark, the sculpture of God the Father and the paintings
of Strahov Madonna and St. Barbara are among the most treasured
parts of the Strahov Picture Gallery collection

St. Barbara by the Master of Vyšší Brod, works by the Master of the Litoměřice Altarpiece, the Doksany Ark, and other artworks documenting the maturity of Gothic art in Bohemia as well as other parts of Europe.

The Gothic component of the exhibition is followed by examples of the works of Lucas Cranach the Elder (Master IW), Bartholomeus Spranger, Joseph Heintz the Elder, and Dutch and Flemmish masters of the 16th and 17th centuries. The numerous collections of Bohemian Baroque are represented by Karel Škréta, Jan Kryštof Liška, Michael Halbax, and Petr Brandl. The painters on display further include Václav Vavřinec Reiner, Antonín Kern, František Xaver Palko, Norbert Grund, Franz Anton Maulbertsch, František Xaver Procházka, and August Piepenhagen. The copy of Albrecht Dürer's *'The Feast of the Rose Garlands'* is an admired work of art. The original, owned by the monastery until 1795, is at the National Gallery in Prague today.

The mid 17th century portal is decorated with English clocks dating from around 1750

STRAHOV
Monastery

Published for the Strahov Library
of the Royal Premonstratensian Canonry of Strahov
by Jitka Kejřová,
V Ráji Publishers
as its 177th publication; 72 pages, 72 photographs.
First edition, Prague, 2008
Text © Evermod Gejza Šidlovský, O. Praem, 2008
Photographs © Miloslav Hušek, 2008
Archives of the Royal Premonstratensian Canonry Strahov (pp. 41, 42, 43)
Translation © Petr Kurfürst, 2008
Cover and Graphic Design: Ota Kaplan
Responsible Editors: Markéta Stehlíková and Jindřich Kejř
Printed by Východočeská tiskárna, s. r. o., Sezemice, 2008
ISSN: 1213-6514 (Bibliotheca Strahoviensis)
ISBN: 978-80-86758-53-3

www.strahovmonastery.cz